HAIKU IN APRIL

little grief's hidden
in the bass of the skull split
can disappear now

briefs freeze the legs
in a cool chill on my haira
. HAIKU FOR SPRING

the muddy night bleeds
...rivers wash till morning comes
and the heart bleeds pain

Easter has roots here!
love rises from death Sundays
...siTHREE HAIKU

A big plate of fish
fried up to celebrate feasts
near the end of Spring

the moon looks hugely
down on our diming world now
the sun is old and tired

DAWN HAIKU

the calm of the day
is the morning twilight now
...summer shines for me

THURSDAY HAIKU

the stereo melts
into song and sings softly
morning songs to me

CLIMATE HAIKU

the planet will cool
...the carbon rate goes down now
,,,the species return

NUMBING HAIKU

frost covers me up
...mystical snows of my mind
...painlesss and cooling

love haiku

i sink into bed
hug my pillow like the niight
...think of you always

EMOTIVE HAIKU

fhe stroke took me up
...bloomed me...a shivering bum
....I lie awake nights

TWO SEX HAIKU

big arsed barbara
thighs around tight to my crotch
right in my two lips

the hills swim like her
woman of my dreams she was
...pastoral beauty

HAIKU WITH FRECKLES

when we are young girls
trapped in our minds in the dark
wondering the like

HAIKU FOR SOUTH

cane and cotton bloom
the eyes look white with red spots
...or far gone....downcast

MOVE HAIKU

traditions crumble
we go far and fast away
until we rest safely

SLUDGE HAIKU

muddy manners here
....the golden earth mixes up well
smells like earth and dung

COLD HAIKU

all night we shiver
surface of bodies to sheets
wishing we could hide

SWEET HAIKU

small as a handfull
big as a mountain as well
...the soul sweet i love

FALLING HAIKU

weakly plead mercy

from the abyss that fails you
deeply wounding life

STINKIN HAIKU

the anal canal
full of its crap and sex stuff
...hidden needs amass

SERANADE HAIKU

lilting notes expand
the universe unfolds so
...love is in the air!

RELIEF HAIKU

dead summer things end
in sweltering heat which lasts long
into the darkening

SOFT MUSIC HAIKU

religious notes sing
in choruses made to rember
...but so softly now

STICK HAIKU

stick like snake in mind
...is it stick or snake in mind
...only soul knows answere

GOD HAIKU

I need him alot
I am lost without him too!
Is the world ending?

MAMA GIRL HAIKU

the milk in the breast
and the gentley stroking look
...cushions for my head!

ANXIOUS HAIKU

nerves fire like bullets
the eyes swell redden alot
...love is suffuse now

CONFUSED HAIKU

confusion in mind
the hair stands electricly up
...everything is dumb

DRUNK HAIKU

drinking up the night
....a way to cream your brains up
in a toast to pride

HERO HAIKU

big balls and glory
fade with age to the uglies
...an old man sits, farts

LOVE DUST HAIKU

words full of sex now
...fill the void of our being
with the dust of peace

VIXEN HAIKU

rancid butter butt
...the lies she tells to move things
....they end up in hell

CHANGE HAIKU

my old self is gone
i am dumb but i am happy
watching things evolve

SOMEONES BIG HAIKU

rachel is perfect sweet
my hand trembles at her touch
sometimes she gets soft

PINCH ME HAIKU

its too good to be
so true it is....really great
i could float off too

CREAM HAIKU

the best of the fat
the thickest richest pornogragh
the real find you know

SUMMER ANXIETY HAIKU

you burn up real bad
but inside there is a sheer cool
frost outside where you gaze

COFFEE HAIKU

tastes delicious good
but it makes the heart race real fast
a little crazier

MOVING HAIKU

we make it away
we escape with breath to share
to a nice place there

BAD NERVES HAYKU

blood pressure soars up
talk gets messed up and confused
i want to sleep agatn

EMERGENCY ROOM HAIKU

all night you sweated
in a cold chair starving up
till you'd leave and die

MY HERO HAIKU

you stayed through hard pain
till they treated you...for me
and kitty you stayed

DOZING HAIKU

late at night music
plays with shinvers under fam
....in august heat here

MY APARTMENT HAIKU

no dusty corners
no room for desparing smudge
...just warm and cumfy

PHEONIX HAIKU

explosion to flame
in later years of living
where world ends like this

LINK HAIKU

line to line thingss join
in videos virtual real
light which lies to you

BIG SPACE HAIKU

the apartment has
room for sofas and artwork
and views of nature

LIVE HAIKU

rachel has to live
...enough of her medical hurt
....she must live and do well

SUMMER HAIKU

time to bake in sun

limp along decaying walkways
into a heater

RETIREMENT HAIKU

not from work but grief
stress does not sustain to well
...Hell is hot and cold

AIRCOOL HAIKU

the ice of the air
...artifice over heating
...silent illusion

NATURE ESCAPES ME HAIKU

so calming yet full
so alive with sex and hope
...perhaps it is false

VET CRAZY HAIKU

the cat howls in fright
his eyes dilate he sees fear
later falls asleep

TIME CRAZY HAIKU

we wait all in here
die during the minutes to
...the vet looks haggard

HOT HAIKU

the northwest has it
a swell of temperature
people cooked alive

WAKE UP HAIKU

do people not know
the earth is dying from heat
...surely now they know

TREES HAIKU

nature breathes, sweats rain
I am in awe by window
views of my garden

HAPPINESS HAIKU

please be happy now
we can manage our joy, art
kiss eternity

DISABLED HAIKU

i try to think, walk
help in small ways with leaving
but to no avail

THE SALE HAIKU

this huge house I love

...this relic of a small past
...away and gone now

LUCKY GUY hIKU

I was lukiest
when things fell apart. The world
baked like dough to bread

GNATS HAIKU

gnats swarm in the sun
the day is itchy rotten
the apple stinks too much

ELECTRIC RED HAIKU

the moon in autumn
turn to an orange balloon
in the hot fall sky

KNOW NOTHING HAIKU

what do we know now?
have we learned how to reason?
my head in the trash

FRAIL HAIKU

frail figures dance up
a storm for imagination
on the willow branches

END HAIKU

tiny end of living
in the space our embrace
...lucky man he was

WEIRD HAIKU

I am a limp dick
I am morally dirty
i am not myself

YOU HAIKU

pussies are hot too
be yourself when you love me
feel like dirt, lovely

TREADING WATER HAIKU

superficial steps
pushiing the walker this way
toward the hungry mail

LUCKY DAY HAIKU

frighterning...the miles
between the house and this place
....apartment in clouds

SHEIK HIKU

rubber bonnet on
the woman killer's helmet
....dying for allah

IDIOT HAIKU

presidential dumb!
big barbarian stupid
making fun of lame

flute haiku

jazz among the flat
apartments of chapel hill
blooming from the swamp

LYING HERE HAIKU

dreams sail by on clouds
love and sex sound like thunder
while you sink on down

RADIO TALK Haiku

the radio talks
the news is terrible but
also acurate

NEWS HAIKU

I stay awake now
listen to the news at night
and wonder things to

WASTE HAIKU

plastics abound here
all over the ocean too
they suffocate us

FALL HAIKU

I am heat tender
the sun bakes me bad these days
i sleep in aircool

BLOOD HAIKU

relation of genes
...hefty opening of veins
...early memory

INSECT HAIKU

six legged friendlies
...foreign in looks they seem like
but so alke they are

SUMMER BREEZE HAIKU

wafting lullibies
wake me to a bliue afternoon
dazzle me dreamy

INTINCT HAIKU

I have none, am mindless
but without a direction
....the chaos of the cosmos

the sickness haiku

my head is stuffed up
pain killers don't work that well

music and poems distract

SEPTEMBER HAIKU

frosty days creep in
in summer's elongation
to oblivion

HAUNT HAIKU

ghosts are coming here
they transcend form spacially
and quickly vanish

TWO HAIKU

morning frosted feilds
this way until winter arrived
bringing nighttime skys

the dark days come here
they swallow us alive too
coat everything darkly

TIRED OUT HAIKU

fatigue bleeds on us
...love is like that... it hurts you
we long for sleep now

BLUE MONDAY HAIKU

violons wept then
sunday turned to dry monday
on the radio

weekday haiku

Slpping through the week
mindlessly oblivious to
all of the things sinking

last haiku of the fall

the leaves don't shiimmer
...they bearly turn quite yellow
but the season is here

how precious the cold haiku

i dont want this burn
...this sweatshop of all the days
into a bleak future

EARLY FALL MORNING HAIKU

nothingness echoes
outside in the wind from us
here inside our thoughts

MENTAL NOTES OF COLD HAIKU

the planet warrms to fear
...the cold is not terrible
...the cold kiss of air

FEAR HAIKU

i am paranoid
about the house selling wrongly
...so much at this hour

MOON HAIKU

the moon is the sign
of loves horrible falling
...so bleak and lonely

waft haiku

love laighs in Autumn
laughs with wind through leaves shaking
laughs and weeps a lot

SMALL SINS HAIKU

small sins make us sing
like humble dust amonga trees

we sing and laugh now

FALL HAIKU

leaf crisp! autumn bends
toward us is a wrinkled kiss
everything is good

COOL HAIKU

the cooling is great
the fall comes upon us now
Autumn is here

EMOTIONAL PAIN HAIKU

in love there is pain
there is a lightly blown breeze
in the autumn trees

EUINOX HAIKU

her love is immense
her coat sparkles up to us
autumn shivers up

stuck haiku

days shiver blandly
my anxiety terrifies me
i am stuck like glue

OLD CAT HAIKU

i am confronted
...a cat each time we argue
...old and tired...lumpy

WHOLE HEART HAIKU

I am your grin now
...what you laugh at knowingly
your eyes sparkling up

IKU

we had exploded then
into each others arms again
duribg a chilly fall

LATE IN LIFE HAIKU

we find then again
late in life love family
again we meamt them

SHIVERING DAWN HAIKU

corridors of light
suffuse the darkness early
with falls pronouncements

CHAPEL HILL HAIKU

your strangeness completes
my feelings of death inside
this strange twilight life

THE CHILL HAIKU

frost tingles today
the warming globe tilts spacewise
into the center

SHIVER HAIKU

i tremble at cold
the dead icicles drip down
the warmth is much worse

FRATRICIDAL RIGHTS HAIKU

pointing guns on black crowds
breathing poison breath iin food stores
without masked blockage

NERVOUS SLEEP HAIKU

up and down pacing
the hallways and corridors
of dreamless image

SHIVERING HAIKU

the cold comes in fall
lightly we tremble from cold
and the dark surrounds

SONG HAIKU

choral voices richly
sing the heart of us tonight
move like autumn leaves

WEEKEND HAIKU

Public Radio
plays music on the weekends
old timey good stuff

LIE IN BED HAIKU

listen to the best
news and music on the radio
not for money stuff

THE FROST OF DAWN HAIKU

silently cold comes
against the blues of friday
...love, lonely sinking

FALL MUSIC HAIKU

listen to the hard blues
of night in autumn freezing
love and lonely souls

FRATERNAL HAIKU

these labours last on
in the heart where they appear
in fall where they come

LONGING FOR SLEEP HAIKU

night will not last long
...that precious darkness ceases
that lovely numbness

THE NUMB HAIKU

in a kind of numb
end to us, the days warm up,
we doze off this way

ANXIETY HAIKU

chilled nuts in the pit
of the earthen stomuch seem
a normal thing now

FRIDAY BLISS HAIKU

muaic all evening
folk blues into the night now
lie in bed and sing

WEEKEND RADIO HAIKU

joy enourmous now
the night sings with the radio
...love is in the air

BARE FEET IN THE COLD HAIKU

I travel outside
stumble with my crippled legs
turn the lock clockwise
SHIVERING SIDEWAYS HAIKU

I am tired and cold
but i oerservere this way
come in to the light

THE SINS OF THE FATHERS HAIKU

we have ruined things
...the planet warns in bad ways
we sew a bad seed

RENEWAL HAIKU

things are getting good
slewly the effort is made
money where mouth is

QUIET RAIN HAIKU

pitter patter here
the slow drops of the season
lonely distant sound

NUMB AS DRUGS HAIKU

like the hospital
this quiet room in the rain
love waiting for death

YEARS PASS HAIKU

slow jazz meanders
so the river flows onward
dim llights capure us

LOVE IS SO HARD HAIIKU

nothing matters more
than that vast abyss wich calls
meeting likewise here

STARS FLOAT HAIKU

up there they float on
in the black heavens liike chalk
on a board etched there

LOVE IS BURNT HAIKU

love cooks in this heat
blisters with hot house sickness
in these, their final days

PORCH HAIKU

do you breathe in air
in the forest as i do
from my porch us there

DEATH HAIKU

black wood and black earth
in the forest of my dreams
as i fall asleep

THE COOL NIGHTS THAT COME HAIKU

terrible night comes
cold as ice our salvation
much like outer space

ROCK AND ROLL NIGHT HAIKU

this saturday night
will be bathed in music now
live rcck and roll plays

PRAYER HAIKU

god gives welcome here
blesses your meditation
on issues of peace

PRAYER 2 HAIKU

god liistens to us
our hearts are welcomed by him
inside of his arms

SHORT DAY HAIKU

frost snaps the branches
morning is hyonotic here
inside chapel hill

BREATHE IN HAIKU

breathe in the fall air
nuts adorn the yard these days
love sleeps eternally

THANKSGIVING HAIKU

this thursday along
with the poetry, stories
and the music too

THANK GOD HAIKU

thanks to the essence
we celebrate earth nature
along with good things

FIVE am HAIKU

at this blackenwd hour
where thunder stalks outside
...the deep muffled shade

WIND HAIKU

vague distances here
....music like tin ratling sad
...the humming sleeps now

CRIPPLE HAIKU

the limbs strain to walk
..ache in throbbing srides along
the pathways of fall

SIGNATURE HAIKU

x mark the spot here
not an x but a sleppy
zero on the line

SIGN YOUR NAME HAIKU

...but what is a name?
an indicator of my
presence here on earth

STOLEN HAIKU

fleeced by midnight's swirl
...stolen by the magnitude
of blackness late night

VINEGAR HAIKU

your cunt smells so good
...pregnant with the itch of dawn
...flowers of the bath

DISAPPEAR HAIKU

we will disappear
not from cold but too much warmth
into vacant space

MOUNTAIN HAIKU

winter mountain top
...cabin built and steaming up
...deer chassing shadows

OLD CAT HAIKU

i am confronted

the whole mad swirl of everything to come begins now!

What's New
Poetry Forum
Short Stories
Mad Gallery
Open Mic
Submissions

Sam Silva

Three Haiku: Sale, Lucky, Gnats
featured in the poetry forum October 21, 2021 :: 0 comments

THE SALE

this huge house I love

...this relic of a small past
...away and gone now

***
LUCKY GUY

I was luckiest
when things fell apart. The world
baked like dough to bread

***
GNATS

gnats swarm in the sun
the day is itchy rotten
the apple stinks too much
editors note:

Just as life comes in short bursts; our luck can turn on the sale of a gnat. – mh clay
LIGHT HAIKU
featured in the poetry forum July 19, 2021 :: 0 comments

a light diffuses black
..it lathers the sky that way
...clouds spread like thunder
editors note:

A light lather is a close shave. – mh clay

FRANKENSTEIN
featured in the poetry forum April 30, 2021 :: 0 comments

Places where the dead are plugged
...electric to all passion's core
wandering the peasant groves
...confused by an uncertain brain
and terrorizing man and beast
and women also
like a boar
searching warmth
in fear of fire.
Destruction in desire's feast
the way the dead can feel desire!!
editors note:

Like this, we grope our grove, in search of life's bright bolt. – mh clay

An achy nervousness
among pandemic days
while summer turns toward Fall
and the politics of madness
in the election of it all

and my own old age decays
dully for its sadness
like some disease which slays

with a sleep that fills our eyes
with an image on TV
of dreamy dreamy hot fires
in the skies.
editors note:

Flat screen, flat deal! We are what we watch. – mh clay

THE LOVE BOND
featured in the poetry forum November 7, 2020 :: 0 comments

See we are ancient already! We are marble
carved and sealed to fortressed stone
inseparable the way we aged together
and glistening in our polish
like one of your starry paintings.

Or an old rustic house
grown out as one toward the woodland.
We live in the same skin
shelter under each other's locks.

I look out the window of your brilliant eyes
and see and give utterance for the world
eternally brand new!
editors note:

Yes! Give utterance! – mh clay

act in the face
which he could not stand

so he puffed up a cloud
in his glacial station
to obscure that cruel beauty
of the land.
editors note:

In this case, smoke 'em when you DON'T... – mh clay

ART AS THE GHOSTLY SOPRANO
featured in the poetry forum June 15, 2020 :: 0 comments

This is the love among the dead
...these are those high operatic notes
...that gorge of meat and wine and bread
...that private castle leaking hope, despair,
the two the same in desperate sighs

encased in predatory motes
to keep away the warlike herds
of Mongols milking mares and goats
with lost dreams much like lullabies
composed by angels

....without words...
editors note:

And, yet, we must sing them... – mh clay

THE MUSIC OF THE OCEAN'S COAST
featured in the poetry forum April 10, 2020 :: 0 comments

Midnight longing for God and Heaven
Horns of sweet jazz for Jesus
in the missionary night.

Converting bats like me to bliss,
bugs, to that kiss of divinity
...the lucky and beloved to a sigh
alike the sea
editors note:

Sing contentment in every key. – mh clay

A CITY LIKE BERLIN
featured in the poetry forum January 20, 2020 :: 0 comments

Fire at night! Fire
in the coal dark cold
of an ice like desire
that chokes the eyes
like wicked smoke
under shrouded skies
and bilious smog

...and a breathy toke
on a deadly drug
which sells the soul
which howls like a dog
in lightning storms
against thunder sounds
whose big guns bellow a hundred rounds
on our crumbling station
our crumbling forms
our tired nation
our hell-bent choir.

Fire at night....such wicked fire!
editors note:

Public works or public outrage? What's happening in your city? – mh clay

TIRED MEN OF THE ASHES
featured in the poetry forum November 4, 2019 :: 0 comments

The manifest of my dreams
in spring
is written cool, bland,
lyrically lazy
about the green shrubbery
and the yellow brown roses
come ugly upon a trailer park Easter

...a bit of leafy stem
sticks its head above
the loam

and this is our Jesus!, our poetry!
editors note:

Jesus in every flower. Resurrection in every Spring. – mh clay

1
2
3
?

A bit about Sam: Sam Silva has poetry in print magazines including, but not limited to Samisdat, The ECU Rebel, Sow's Ear, The American Muse, St. Andrews Review, Dog River Review, Third Lung Review, Main St. Rag, Charlotte Poetry Review, Parnasus...most (but not all) of these magazines are now defunct. For the past four years his magazine portfolio has grown by and large on line including Rio Del Arts, Megaera, Big Bridge, Views unplugged, Comrade Magazine, Ken Again and at least thirty others. Over the years four small presses have published a total of nine chapbooks by Sam Silva ...these, being Third Lung Press, M.A.F. Press, Alpha Beat Press, Trouth Creek Press. Brown and Yale Universities solicited many of these chapbooks for their libraries. These chapbooks were well received in newspaper reviews by Shelby Stephenson, Ron Bayes, Steve Smith, and the late poet laureate of North Carolina Sam Ragan. Silva has ebooks available without cost at Physikgarden.com. He has well over 300 poems archived in online magazines. He was nominated a total of seven times by three small presses and has a full length collection of poetry called Eating and Drinking based on a royalties contract signed with Bright Spark Creative available for order at any online bookstore and has other full length poetry books available at amazon.com. Three spoken word CDs of Sam Silva's have been marketed through CDBaby.

What's New
Poetry
Short Stories
Mad Gallery
Open Mic
Submissions
Merch
Contact

© 2021
...a cat each time we argue
...old and tired...lumpy

WHOLE HEART HAIKU

I am your grin now
...what you laugh at knowingly
your eyes sparkling up

Empty Mirros 2

MY FRIENDS AND I, WE STOLE THE SUMMER

My friends and I, we stole the summer
and its rain
in stumbling secret conversation
about the brilliant ways of the city

...all of its joy
and all of its pain!

In a little room I call my friends
and speak of a journey which never ends
while they all disappear
one by one

...and I may be left
...ah what a Pity!
to share my words
with the setting Sun.

PROLITERIAN VALUES

Eyes glazed in dumb fatigue
...and thoughts behind
were ill defined
...a thick morass which sank a league
to coral forests made for Hell.

How does a turnip learn to bleed?
How are the sharks and stars aligned
for this great feast of human greed?

But in the end they are!, they are
the destiny of humankind!

WORDS ARE THE ONE SMALL THING I TRIED

Words tend to fail me!
Outside a forest of ivy climbs
the weedy hills of our yard. Entombed
in dust a nickel shines
upon these mounds and gullies
where come the Fall red sunlight bloomed
on yesteryears
and will, for years to come.

The older years are so good
…the eyes upon my lover's art inside
see golden
as the hands in the dark feel wood.

Words are the one small thing I tried
while such visions strike me dumb!

ESSENTIAL DREAMS AND ART

Medieval grace
in dancing marks
in fish all full of color
in the market place
or under coral waves
among the sharks

it all comes to our passion
and it all comes to our graves
and matter barely matters
in this, my lover's sweetly abstract style

a portrait of the self, mine or hers
is what she eats and what she saves
where still lifes heap the platters
with much more than a sense of passing fashion
but with deep flesh
and even deeper soul

…what could be left?
…we are but curs
curling in our cresh
and desperate for our God!

We are but orphan lambs bereft
…and, at evening,
hold each other

….fall asleep and nod.

PARANOID ORPHAN FANTASY

The smell of smoke and methane gas!
...a haunt of trailer ghosts which kill,
inflame. seduce
those wild weeds growing in the grass
and women
of a lesser will
...a pin prick lessens all such pain
for all such boys grown old too soon
and all such girls
who likewise pass
a test to leave all life behind
and stumble up a concrete step
and enter metal's thin disguise
and sit in chairs with cigarettes
and gaze upon a midnight rain
and gaze, in fact. beyond such clouds
to life beyond the far side of the Moon!

FROM ONE OF HELL'S MINOR CIRCLES

Smoker puffs for fifty years
trailing aromatic thoughts
makes a dead weight of his tears
barely sighs when all is said
...barely sighs but mostly coughs!

Ceremonies of the dead
...how to live not being there!
Passion's plum...more wine than bread.
But ah! the lovers in their love!
Not even mad sex can compare!
How could you not be tender?, you
who live among each other's love

instead of dreaming such sad words
among the flowers and the dew!

A CAROLINA COLLEGE TOWN

I was a pig cooled in mud
....living near the artists and politicos
with my one ac unit in the window
of a room which was half the apartment
and smelled of a thousand sweaty rags.

And I would write and chain smoke all Summer long
except for the blessing of cool and windy evenings
outside of the shed on a stump....till the stars came
out, and assumed the same wild pathos
which carried my voice...

CHEISRMAS ON CONTENTNIA ST
With private moods of calm desire
nights beside a wooden fire
in winters made of long ago
whose youth endured such paths through snow
whose rented room was destiny
...small gifts beneath a naked tree!
Share on Twitter
Share on Facebook
Sam Silva

Sam Silva has published over 150 poems in print magazines, including Sow's Ear, The ECU Rebel, Pembroke Magazine, Samisdat, St. Andrew's Review, Charlotte Poetry Review, Main Street Rag and others. Has published at least 300 poems in online journals including Jack Magazine, Comrades, Megaera, Poetry Super Highway, physik garden, Ken again, -30-, Fairfield Review, Foliate Oak, and dozens of others. He is a frequent contributor to Empty Mirror.

His chapbooks have been published by three small presses, and his work has been nominated for a Pushcart Prize seven times. Bright Spark Creative of Wilimington published his first full-length book, EATING AND DRINKING.

He now has many books and chapbooks available at lulu.comsamsilva54 and as books available at Amazon. His spoken word poetry is available at the major digital markets such as Apple iTunes. Follow him on Twitter @samsilva1954.

Empty Mirror 1

a literary magazine

About

Five poems by Sam Silva

Sam Silva
Minimum Pink - Denise Enck
image credit: Denise Enck
MUSICAL STILL LIFE WITH COMPUTER

Guitar serenade
...the plucked harp of my soul
lingers as well
in the cave I made
of my heart with its hole

echoing through computer wires
with their flickering lights
like electric fires

.

WHAT SAY YOU COUNTRY BOY?

Bland things now! Bland and dull and easy!
The painless ardor of a mind entombed
by cigarettes and old fashioned cough syrup
...the bottle and the butt
suckled and consumed
to distinctions made in circular smoke
and wandering thoughts
whose narration comes to dip and drift
in summers long ago
and more recently in Winter

...friends and lovers! Miracles
and tragic loss!
now even as the steam exhales
and death trains move away from here,

The child released his future
and a vagrant began his wanderings
down paths as different
and decayed

as were the ways

of such an age as this.

WHAT A THING LIKE WINTER SUGGESTS

Like a cat huddled
among the cold weather briars
…four even paws
and a ball of fur
shaken ruffled by wind

I, in the quiet nuance of my words
in this Southern U.S. house in a field
full of winter birds
have muddled and shrunk
in a frigid place

where at night
with its stars and its bars
and its dim gas fires
…why, nights like this cause
the blankets to be peeled
where no one sinned
and yet, sin we did on this lonely planet
in outer space!

AMONG THE DEAD THINGS WHICH WE DOUBT

Among the dead things which we doubt
religions of the dead devour
the kiss of life
with their bleak flower

...that old gray heaven like a choir
of static voices
rasping out
the essence of all dryness
...like a throat on fire
which longs to whisper
...not to shout!

AROUND THE CANDLE AT MIDNIGHT

My ache for you is existential
...your pores breathe life in a painting
and the days are getting furtive and hungry
against the loud bebop of my computer streaming
or the cool jazz grown to a list of lazy facts
parallel to this Carolina winter outside.

Cocoons envelop my passion!
And a cold and spiteful world surrounds
...you paint for me
like our years of lovemaking
an image both crisp and still and perfect
and yet so serenely celebrant
in laughing the language of light

made of body
and spirit
framed and held up.
Share on Twitter
Share on Facebook
Sam Silva

Sam Silva has published over 150 poems in print magazines, including Sow's Ear, The ECU Rebel, Pembroke Magazine, Samisdat, St. Andrew's Review, Charlotte Poetry Review, Main Street Rag and others. Has published at least 300 poems in online journals including Jack Magazine, Comrades, Megaera, Poetry Super Highway, physik garden, Ken again, -30-, Fairfield Review, Foliate Oak, and dozens of others. He is a frequent contributor to Empty Mirror.

His chapbooks have been published by three small presses, and his work has been nominated for a Pushcart Prize seven times. Bright Spark Creative of Wilimington published his first full-length book, EATING AND DRINKING.

He now has many books and chapbooks available at lulu.comsamsilva54 and as books available at Amazon. His spoken word poetry is available at the major digital markets such as Apple iTunes. Follow him on Twitter @samsilva1954.

Author: Sam Silva Tags: poetry Category: Poetry March 13, 2015
You might also like:
Berthusen -- D. Enck
Three new poems by Mark Young
ten mile / credit: d.e.
Three poems by Linda E. Chown
gramophone
Two poems by Benjamin Smith
photo copyright http://www.sxc.hu/profile/dlritter

A CAROLINA COLLEGE TOWN

I was a pig cooled in mud
....living near the artists and politicos
with my one ac unit in the window
of a room which was half the apartment
and smelled of a thousand sweaty rags.

And I would write and chain smoke all Summer long
except for the blessing of cool and windy evenings
outside of the shed on a stump....till the stars came
out, and assumed the same wild pathos
which carried my voice...

A CLASSICAL SOUTHERN SUMMER

Bethoven lifted the notes in his symphonies
higher than miles
...alone on my rocking chair
in a cool indoor room
I ruminate over the Sun as it sets
in a time of broiling hot July
which burries the Spring in a tomb.

CAROLINA COOL

So many snippets
of ashed out Summer remain
...and yet, cool Fall comes!

Rain and fog settle
...introduce me to Fall Swamps
...cool among the pine.

Till Halloween bleeds
into November,and then
waters chill to ice.

CITY ON A SOUTHERN SWAMP

Summer's heat broils on
whose sky's ablaze come evening
...the beer joints and the honky tonks
alleviate such scalding thirst
where eyeballs are about to burst
like water from a frail god's side

They carry love's weight like a cross!
these tee shirt girls
with strings of pearls
...the cat that curls
...the goose that honks
where midnight cooks a line of cars
devoted to the word within
as are these women of the night
and soldiers
sitting numb...in bars.

EMOTIVE HAIKU

fhe stroke took me up
...bloomed me...a shivering bum
....I lie awake nights

A CAROLINA HALOWEEN

The horn of the wind
blue jazz on that October night
where blue Billy lay
and Lisa sinned
and spirit passed the liquor tinned
from carnalities which kiss the mouth
of every witchey virgin child
in this sweet corner
of the South...

WHERE WE GOT OUR COOL

Jazz within the sky
...gold upon this purple swamp
...this bebop swank
of lullaby
where angels sell their poetry
for that treasure of a girl's sweet thigh
thrust upward
on the dew and damp
where river bank
meets lullaby.

Oh God!...hot days have left us here
to broil until the seasons cool

that measure, with an Autumn tear
on the face of every fool
who syncopates his joy with grief

and air conditioned Winter bears
its icicles
upon a frozen leaf!
MEMORIES OF A SPRING EUTHANASIA

The jazz from horn and piano
flows and trembles
in those greedy notes of this ensemble
of wind and percussive
cussed chords in the grief of summer
glowing hot in late July

…a tear forms in my eye!
In my eye, this afternoon
bleeding art beyond a June
and whispered with a storm that day
when the dog of our dreams had gone away…

DOROTHY'S OTHER STORY

Among the highborn women of Oz
…frosty knickers
in November's early Winter
on such a golden highway
marking frozen dreams
and frigid sex
in that fire breathing dragon's ancient
stately cause
handed down

from Tyrannosaurus Rex

...and given to a clown
for making all of the ancient lizards laugh
...a strange low burning thing!,
this cool fire
barely touched by warm desire!
this icy wine carafe
held within the fire circle's ring!
IN A BRIEF TIME MUCH LIKE INNOCENCE

Jazz of the hot sweet lullaby nectar
of summer and its wild flowers
bloomed in tumult
of yellow and red
upon the fields of the living.

A few August storms will shed rain
in the future weeks
...roll on into September
and then cool.

Puff and wind of dandelion brain
when the dry of Autumn arrives
to scatter scarecrow seed...oh senseless fool!
Share on Twitter
Share on Facebook
Sam Silva

Sam Silva has published over 150 poems in print magazines, including Sow's Ear, The ECU Rebel,
Pembroke Magazine, Samisdat, St. Andrew's Review, Charlotte Poetry Review, Main Street Rag
and others. Has published at least 300 poems in online journals including Jack Magazine,
Comrades, Megaera, Poetry Super Highway, physik garden, Ken again, -30-, Fairfield Review,
Foliate Oak, and dozens of others. He is a frequent contributor to Empty Mirror.

His chapbooks have been published by three small presses, and his work has been nominated
for a Pushcart Prize seven times. Bright Spark Creative of Wilimington published his first full-
length book, EATING AND DRINKING.

He now has many books and chapbooks available at lulu.comsamsilva54 and as books available
at Amazon. His spoken word poetry is available at the major digital markets such as Apple
iTunes. Follow him on Twitter @samsilva1954.

www.ingramcontent.com/pod-product-compliance
Lightning Source LLC
Chambersburg PA
CBHW080723120726
48001CB00010B/3126